Rick Gage

DOWNLOAD

God has given you incredible resources.
Learn to use them, so you can grow
strong in Christ!

Published in the United States by Rick Gage Evangelistic Association

Cover design and layout by Seed Studios at seedstudios.com

ISBN: 0-9646473-2-X

TABLE OF CONTENTS

A LETTER FROM RICK

Dear Friend,

I am so excited about your interest in Jesus Christ! If you have recently trusted Him as your Lord and Savior, you're in for the greatest adventure life can offer. If you have been a Christian for awhile, you know exactly what I mean when I say that Christ gives us the most peace and the biggest challenges we can ever experience. And if you're still unsure about how you relate to Jesus, this booklet will help clarify things for you.

When people put their faith in Christ, an amazing thing happens: Their citizenship changes! They are "rescued . . . from the dominion of darkness and brought . . . into the kingdom" of God's Son (Colossians 1:13). Along with their passport, their heart's desires change, too. Instead of selfishly wanting to please only themselves, they now want to please God by following His directions.

I want you to get started right; or if you've already been walking with Christ, I want you to keep going on the right path. You probably have a million questions, and each lesson is designed to answer a lot of those questions. As you read this booklet and the passages from the Bible, ask God to give you light and heart . . . light to understand the truth and a courageous heart to claim His promises and follow His commands. As you spend time with God and with those who love Him, your life will be transformed. And you'll have the incredible thrill of seeing lives changed—including yours!

Sincerely in Christ,

Rick Gage

INTRODUCTION:

CHECK THE TUTORIAL

When you become a Christian, it's like getting a new, powerful software program. It has all kinds of features—so many, in fact, that it takes more than a lifetime to understand them all! The moment you trust Christ as your Lord and Savior, you are "a new creation; the old has gone, the new has come" (2 Corinthians 5:17)! Here are a few of the incredible, new truths in your life:

—All your sins are forgiven: past, present, and future.

—You become a child of God Almighty, the Creator of the universe.

—God's Holy Spirit takes up residence in you.

—God's incredible love and grace are yours to enjoy.

—You can better understand God's Word, the Bible; and it becomes rich and rewarding.

—Your desires gradually change from wanting only selfish pleasures to wanting to honor God and help people.

—Friendships with other Christians bring more fulfillment than any relationships you've ever known.

But the journey of following Christ isn't easy. It's full of wonder, but it's sometimes challenging. It's full of joy, but we sometimes experience heartache over our sins and the sins of others.

I've known lots of young people who embraced Christ, received a new heart from Him, and took their first steps on the path of knowing and loving

Jesus Christ. All of those elements of being a Christian that I just mentioned (the presence and the power of God, purpose in life, rich relationships, etc.) took root in their lives; and they became strong in their faith.

But I've also known some young people who, for some reason, didn't "get it." They started with excitement at camp, a concert, a conference, or a church service; but after a few days or a few weeks, they drifted away. What makes some of us grow strong and some drift away? That's what this booklet is about. We need to learn to use all the tools and resources we've downloaded from Christ. We need to:

—soak up the truth from His Word, so we know what He wants us to do.

—grow in our love for God, so we want what He wants—for ourselves and for others.

—learn to pray with conviction and passion because we realize we are in the throne room of Almighty God, our loving Father.

—hang out with people who genuinely love God, so some of their knowledge and character rubs off on us.

—tell everybody who will listen about the incredible grace of God we've experienced.

Are you ready to learn and experience these things? I sure hope so. Grab a pen or pencil and a Bible that's easy to read. Take time to carefully read each section of the booklet. The Bible verses are written out in the booklet, but you may want to open your Bible and read the paragraphs where these verses are found. That can really help you understand what the passage is saying. Think about your answer to each question; then write your answers. Find a friend to share your answers with and learn from each other.

And don't forget: Ask your Heavenly Father to teach you every step of the way. His Holy Spirit through you will express His love and His forgiveness toward Him, yourself, and others. As you read, write, and take steps to apply what you learn, you'll grow strong in God's grace and nothing will hold you back!

HOW TO BE SURE YOU'RE A CHRISTIAN

"Did I say the right words?"

"Did I really mean what I said to God?"

"What if I can't measure up and live the way I'm supposed to?"

"At the time, I felt really close to God; but now...."

"I don't really feel that different. Maybe it didn't 'take' for me."

Over the years, I've heard people say things like these (and dozens more) in the days and weeks after they trusted Christ as their Savior. Doubts creep in, and most people don't know what to do with them. They want to talk to somebody, but they don't want anybody to know they're confused.

Look at it this way: Trusting Christ is the most monumental change we can ever experience. Our eternal destiny took a 180, and the core of our identity was radically altered...forever! Change often creates uncertainty, so don't be alarmed if you have questions. Internal change also is hard to explain to family and friends who don't understand. If they aren't excited—or worse, if they criticize our decision to follow Christ, those doubts can scream at us!

In this lesson, I want to help you understand how to be sure you're a Christian. This is important, so pay attention! A rock-solid sense of certainty is the operating system for your spiritual life. If you get this running well, you'll be in great shape. But if this isn't running, you'll crash over and over again. I want to talk about three key points: assurance of our salvation, the eternal life Christ promises, and how this certainty changes our desires.

Assurance of Our Salvation

Our confidence that we belong to God and He belongs to us isn't based on saying some magic words or having particular feelings. It's a matter of where we put our trust. If we're trusting in how cool we are, then we're in trouble. But if we have given up on being good enough to earn God's acceptance and we've put our trust in Christ's death on the cross as payment for our sins, we can be absolutely, completely confident that we are God's children!

The Apostle John had a lot to say about being sure of God's love. In the opening sentences of his gospel, he contrasted those who rejected Christ and those who received Him. Then he told us:

"Yet to all who received him, to those who believed in his name, he gave the right to become children of God" (John 1:12).
• What were some reasons you felt the need to receive Him when you trusted Christ as your Savior? _____

_____

_____

Does God want us to be certain of our relationship with Him? You bet He does! In one of his letters, John explained clearly that if our trust is in Christ, we can be completely sure of our salvation. He wrote:

"And this is the testimony: God has given us eternal life, and this life is in his Son. He who has the Son has life; he who does not have the Son of God does not have life. I write these things to you who believe in the name of the Son of God so that you may know that you have eternal life" (1 John 5:11-13).

Did you catch that? "So that you may know." Not think or hope or wonder or guess . . . but "that you may know that you have eternal life."

• What difference does it make for someone to be sure of his or her salvation?_____

_____

_____

• How might certainty (or a lack of certainty) affect our desire to please God, our desire to spend time studying the Bible and praying, and our relationships with other Christians? _____

_____

_____

One of the most powerful chapters in the Bible is Romans 8. Paul begins that chapter by stating clearly that Christ's death on the cross completely cancels out guilt and condemnation for those who have trusted in Him. That's Good News! And he ends the chapter by promising that nothing in the universe can separate us from God's love. He wrote:

"For I am convinced that neither death nor life, neither angels nor demons, neither the present nor the future, nor any powers, neither height nor depth, nor anything else in all creation, will be able to separate us from the love of God that is in Christ Jesus our Lord" (Romans 8:38-39).

Wow! Paul didn't leave anything out, did he? God is committed to love us through the good times and the bad and through every possible situation we encounter.

• Since our sense of certainty of our salvation is based on our faith in God's promises and not particular words or feelings, on a scale of 0 (not at all) to 100 percent (not a shadow of a doubt), how sure are you that you'd go to heaven if you died today? Explain your answer. _____

_____

_____

The Promise of Eternal Life

Some people have the mistaken idea that "eternal life" is just a series of endless days—one boring moment after another. No wonder they aren't too excited about becoming Christians! Instead eternal life is as much about quality as quantity. Jesus said it means having a rich, rewarding, stimulating relationship with Him, the Creator of the universe and the One who loved us enough to die for our sins. It's the adventure of knowing and loving Him, of finding and following His will, and of being His partner in changing the world. That's anything but boring!

Eternal life is a gift from God, and it's as certain as God's grip on us. In one of the most loved passages in John's gospel, Jesus explained:

"My sheep listen to my voice; I know them, and they follow me. I give them eternal life, and they shall never perish; no one can snatch them out of my hand. My Father, who has given them to me, is greater than all; no one can snatch them out of my Father's hand. I and the Father are one" (John 10:27-30).

• According to this passage, how secure is God's gift of eternal life to you and me? Explain the significance of both Jesus and the Father holding us in Their hands._____

_____

_____

_____

Our salvation and eternal life, though, aren't given because we did enough good things to earn God's acceptance. Not at all! Instead, they're gifts of grace in spite of the fact that we don't deserve them. Paul made this point clear to the believers in Ephesus:

"For it is by grace you have been saved, through faith—and this not from yourselves, it is the gift of God—not by works, so that no one can boast" (Ephesians 2:8-9).

• How does the fact that salvation and eternal life are gifts from God—and not earned by our goodness—affect your attitude toward God? Does it make you more thankful? Why or why not? _____

_____

_____

_____

In one of the best-known passages in the Bible, Jesus explained to Nicodemus that the gift of eternal life contrasts with what we actually deserve for our sins: eternal condemnation. Jesus said,

"For God so loved the world that he gave his one and only Son, that whoever believes in him shall not perish but have eternal life. For God did not send his Son into the world to condemn the world, but to save the world through him" (John 3:16-17).

• If you died today and stood before God, what would you say if He asked you, "Why should I let you into Heaven to experience eternal life?" _____

_____

_____

Developing a Desire to Please God

Some of us think of God the way we think of a teacher in a class we don't particularly like (for me, it would be math!). We might do what they tell us to do, but we do only the minimum to get by. The Scriptures, though, explain that our relationship with God is far richer and deeper than with a distant, demanding teacher. He is our Best Friend, the One who saw us in danger and gave His life to rescue us. He is the One who is so powerful that He spoke a word and a hundred billion galaxies were flung into space, but He cares about you and me each and every minute of every day. Amazingly, our attitudes and actions have the capacity to make God happy or sad. Our anger and selfishness—yours and mine—grieve Him; but love, faith, and following His directions make Him smile.

• What difference does it make to realize your attitudes and behavior affect the mood of the God of the universe? _____

_____

_____

If we have even the slightest clue about the immensity of God's great love, it will radically change our lives. Experiencing His love and grace is like fuel for a space shuttle launch—so powerful that it overcomes natural forces around us! Paul explained the power of this experience to the Christians in Corinth:

"For Christ's love compels us, because we are convinced that one died for all, and therefore all died. And he died for all, that those who live should no longer live for themselves but for him who died for them and was raised again" (2 Corinthians 5:14-15).
• In these verses, Christ's compelling love causes people to stop living selfishly and to live for Him. Give some examples of what this truth might mean in the lives of Christians your age? And in your own life?

_____

_____

_____

One of the reasons we logically choose to please God instead of selfishly pleasing ourselves is that Jesus paid an awful price for our forgiveness and eternal life when He died on the cross. That realization affects how we see ourselves and how we respond to every situation in life. Paul applied this truth to sexual sin in his first letter to the Corinthians:

"Flee from sexual immorality. All other sins a man [or a woman] commits are outside his body, but he who sins sexually sins against his own body. Do you not know that your body is a temple of the Holy Spirit, who is in you, whom you have received from God? You are not your own; you were bought at a price. Therefore honor God with your body" (1 Corinthians 6:18-20).
• Read these verses again carefully, and describe the motivations Paul gives for following God's command to be sexually pure.

_____

_____

_____

• Are these motivations meaningful to you? Why or why not?

_____

_____

_____

Love for God ... and obedience to God's commands—the two go hand-in-hand. In fact, as we obey because we love Him, we experience even more of God's love and presence. Jesus explained this powerful dynamic:

"Whoever has my commands and obeys them, he is the one who loves me. He who loves me will be loved by my Father, and I too will love him and show myself to him" (John 14:21).

• What are some specific things you know God commands you to do (or not do)? _____

_____

_____

_____

• Though you may not feel like obeying God, you can choose to respond to His love for you and please Him by doing what He wants you to do. According to this passage, what is Jesus' promise to you if you do that?_____

_____

_____

_____

Wrap It Up

• What truths in this lesson have encouraged you the most? _____

_____

_____

_____

• How have the principles about assurance, eternal life, and pleasing God helped your faith grow stronger? _____

_____

_____

_____

• Are there some questions that have come to mind during this lesson? Write them here. Who can give you wise input about these questions?

_____

_____

_____

Warning: When we are starting on the path to know and love Christ, our enemy, Satan, often tries to get us off track any way he can. He may try to make you feel really strange about God or the Bible. He may cause you to have conflict with another person. Or he may use criticism from your old friends to cause you to doubt your faith. Whatever he tries to do, be alert and fight back! Talk to a trusted Christian friend to get some strong support and insight. Don't let anything stop you from knowing and loving Christ!

WALK WITH THE WISE

As I look back at my life and as I have watched thousands of young people over the years, I've seen a particular principle of Scripture lived out over and over again. In the book of Proverbs, Solomon wrote, "He who walks with the wise grows wise, but a companion of fools suffers harm" (Proverbs 13:20).

I can't tell you strongly enough how important it is to make good decisions to hang out with wise people. If you do, you'll soak up their wisdom like a sponge. But if you soak up negative, selfish attitudes and follow dumb actions of foolish people, you'll become like them. That cause and effect is what Solomon was talking about, and that's what you and I have seen in the lives of people around us.

"Hanging around wise people," you might be thinking, "Man, that sounds really dull!" I'm not talking about stale religious people who are so stiff that they've lost their creativity and joy. No, I'm talking about people who are thrilled to be loved by Jesus Christ, who experience the joy of knowing Him and the sheer wonder of seeing Him use them to touch other people's lives. That's anything but dull!

In this lesson, I want to focus on the importance of being connected to wise people. We'll look at the quality of these relationships, the church as the body of faithful people, and our privilege to serve God together.

Connections

If you read much in the New Testament, you'll notice how important relationships are to Paul, Peter, Luke, John, and the other writers. Over and over again, they write about the power of friendships in the community of faith. Two words are used over and over again: "one another." Let's look at just a few of the passages that tell us how we can help make each other wise.

John wrote a lot about love: God's love for us and our love for each other. In his first letter, he wrote:

"Dear friends, let us love one another, for love comes from God. Everyone who loves has been born of God and knows God" (1 John 4:7).

• What do you think John means when he says, "love comes from God"? _____

_____

_____

_____

• What are some ways people have shown love to you in the last few days? How have you shown love to others? _____

_____

_____

_____

All of us long to be accepted. We want to belong. That's a basic human need; but far too often, we feel lonely. Others are so absorbed in their own wants and needs that they don't even notice us; or if they do, they don't seem to care. Relationships between believers, though, are based on our experience of God's incredible love and acceptance.

From that tremendous resource in our own lives, we can express love and acceptance to others. Paul wrote to the believers in Rome:

"Accept one another, then, just as Christ accepted you, in order to bring praise to God" (Romans 15:7).

• Do you agree or disagree with the statement, "You can only give out what you've taken in"? How does this principle apply to us accepting others? _____

_____

_____

_____

Let's face it. We're human, and humans sometimes act selfishly. When we hurt each other, we need to forgive. The same principle of experience and expression applies here, too. We can forgive others only as much as we've experienced God's forgiveness for our sins. Paul wrote,

"Be kind and compassionate to one another, forgiving each other, just as in Christ God forgave you" (Ephesians 4:32).

• What are some reasons we don't want to forgive those who have hurt us? _____

_____

_____

• What are some things you can do to appreciate God's forgiveness in your life, so you can more readily forgive people who have hurt you?

_____

_____

_____

• Are there some people you need to forgive? If there are, take time right now to think about God's great forgiveness toward you and then allow the Lord to forgive them through you. _____

_____

_____

_____

God is very realistic. He knows that rich, strong relationships provide the best opportunity to speak truth to each other—even if it hurts sometimes. If we really love each other, we'll have the courage to speak up and say some hard things to warn people to stop messing up their lives. Paul told the Christians at Colossae:

"Let the word of Christ dwell in you richly as you teach and admonish one another with all wisdom..." (Colossians 3:16).

• Describe how our motives are different when we "blow up" at someone who is annoying us and when we "admonish one another with all wisdom." _____

_____

_____

_____

• When is it appropriate to admonish someone? When is it not the right thing to do? What are some guidelines (do's and don'ts) you'd make for yourself as you consider "speaking the truth in love" to someone who is getting off track? _____

_____

_____

_____

The Body of Faithful People

The church is far more than bricks and pews. In fact, many times in history when the church has grown the most were periods when people met in homes or out in the open under trees. The physical building is a great resource, but it's not necessary for God to accomplish His purposes in people's lives.

The church is a group of baptized believers voluntarily joining together for instruction, fellowship, worship, and service. In another of the "one another" passages, the writer to the Hebrews talked about the importance of getting together for these purposes:

"Let us not give up meeting together, as some are in the habit of doing, but let us encourage one another—and all the more as you see the Day approaching" (Hebrews 10:25).

• Is our purpose in going to church to get things from God and people or to give encouragement to people and praise to God? Explain your answer. _____

_____

_____

_____

_____

We enjoy our Bible teachers, and we respect those who lead us; but we need to remember that the Head of the church is Christ Himself. Paul reminded the Colossian believers of that fact:

"And he [Christ] is the head of the body, the church; he is the beginning and the firstborn from among the dead, so that in everything he might have the supremacy" (Colossians 1:18).

• What difference does it make to see Christ, instead of people, as the

Head of the church? _____

_____

_____

Spiritual leaders in the community of faith play a very important role as they follow Christ's directions. They have the responsibility and the privilege of helping believers grow and unbelievers come to faith in Christ. Paul explained their role in his letter to the Ephesians:

"It was he [Christ] who gave some to be apostles, some to be prophets, some to be evangelists, and some to be pastors and teachers, to prepare God's people for works of service, so that the body of Christ may be built up" (Ephesians 4:11-12).

• What are some ways these leaders "build up" your church? _____

_____

_____

_____

• What are their biggest challenges? What are some ways you can help? _____

_____

_____

The Privilege of Serving

Jesus Christ is the Head; and all the rest of us are parts of His body, the church. All of us play a significant role in accomplishing God's purposes. Some of us, though, think we can't contribute much; so we don't even try. Paul addressed that perspective in his letter to the Christians in Corinth. He wrote,

"Now the body is not made up of one part but of many. If the foot should say, 'Because I am not a hand, I do not belong to the body,' it would not for that reason cease to be part of the body" (1 Corinthians 12:14-15).
• What are the dangers in thinking that only certain, visible church leaders are really important to God and His purposes? _____

_____

_____

Just before Jesus ascended to heaven, He gave His followers the sweeping plan to reach the whole world with His message. It's called the Great Commission. It is the greatest challenge the world has ever known, but it is accomplished one person at a time. All of us are parts of the Body of Christ, and all of us are soldiers in God's army. We have the incredible privilege and responsibility to serve Christ by taking His message to our friends, our family, our neighbors, and ultimately to every person on the planet!
• Paul calls you and me "ambassadors" for Christ (2 Corinthians 5:20). What are some specific ways you and I can be really good ambassadors for Him? _____

_____

_____

One of the evidences of our commitment to Christ is how we use the resources He has given us. Some of us think we don't have any resources, but even "poor" people in this country are among the wealthiest in all of history. Our time, talents, and treasures are all gifts from God to be used to honor Him. One of the ways we honor Him is by giving generously to His kingdom. God gives us a promise that He will bless us if we're generous, and He wants us to be thrilled to give. Paul gave us this insight:

"Remember this: Whoever sows sparingly will also reap sparingly, and whoever sows generously will also reap generously. Each man [or woman] should give what he has decided in his heart to give, not reluctantly or under compulsion, for God loves a cheerful giver" (2 Corinthians 9:6-7).

• In your own words, describe this passage's message about the motives and actions of giving to God's kingdom. _____

_____

_____

_____

• Does this passage motivate you to give more? Why or why not?

_____

_____

_____

A Human Billboard

Billboards along the highway are advertisements for all kinds of things. Baptism is a human billboard to tell everybody who will listen that we belong to Jesus Christ. The act of baptism informs our family, friends, and the community that we've made a decision to follow the One who has bought us with His blood and that there's no turning back. Baptism is an outward expression of an inward heart change.

Since the earliest days of the church, believers have been baptized to tell the world about their commitment to Christ. Jesus commanded it in the Great Commission (Matthew 28:18-20), and the early church leaders baptized every person who trusted in Christ—even when thousands responded to the Gospel on a single day! Luke, the author of Acts, wrote about an incredible event:

"Those who accepted his message were baptized, and about three thousand were added to their number that day" (Acts 2:41).

• Have you been baptized? If not, when would be a good time for you to obey Christ's command and become a human billboard to tell the world what He has done for you? _____

_____

_____

Wrap It Up

• What truths in this lesson have encouraged you the most? _____

_____

_____

• How have the principles about spending time with good and godly people, the role of the church, the privilege of serving, and how baptism is an expression of your faith to those around you helped your faith grow stronger? _____

_____

_____

• Are there some questions that have come to mind during this lesson? Write them here. Who can give you wise input about these questions?

_____

_____

_____

_____

PUSH AND PULL

I've heard the Christian life described as "impossible," but I've also heard people say it's "effortless." Some have said it's a tough grind to make hard decisions to honor God, but others say they feel like they are "flying on the wings of an eagle." In my life, some days I get up and want to please God with all of my heart; but other days I just want to please myself.

If we've become Christians and have new hearts, why do we still struggle with temptation? We sometimes find ourselves wondering, "What's wrong?" The answer is: "Probably nothing." We live in the tension between what God has already done in our lives and the fulfillment of what He's going to do when we meet Him face to face.

When we trust Christ as our Lord and Savior, incredible things happen to us. We are delivered from Satan's domain and transferred to God's kingdom. All of our sins are forgiven, and we're set free from the penalty of sin. God's Spirit takes up residence in our bodies, and we become "temples of the Holy Spirit." We have a brand new nature, but the old one is still with us. In fact, our selfish human nature will remain with us until we die or until Christ returns and we meet Him in the air. Professor and author C. S. Lewis commented, "Humans are amphibians—half spirit and half animal. As spirits they belong to the eternal world, but as animals they inhabit time." (He wrote the classic

Mere Christianity as well as *The Chronicles of Narnia* among many other works.)

The presence of these two natures is what gives us the push and pull we experience each day. Paul described this dynamic between our old and new natures when he wrote to the Ephesian Christians:

"...with regard to your former way of life, to put off your old self, which is being corrupted by its deceitful desires; to be made new in the attitude of your minds; and to put on the new self, created to be like God in true righteousness and holiness" (Ephesians 4:22-24).

At every moment of every day, we choose which nature to feed. The one we give time and attention grows stronger, but the one that is rejected and neglected becomes weaker. Until we are with the Lord, both will be calling out to us; but it's up to us to choose which one we nourish.

In this lesson, I want to look at some truths about the role of the Holy Spirit, how to overcome temptation, and how to deal with sin through confession and repentance. Pay attention! This is important stuff!

We're Not Alone

In the last week Jesus spent with His disciples, He explained to them that He was going to be killed, but He would be raised from the dead. In addition, He promised them that after He left the earth, God would send the Holy Spirit to comfort and guide them. (John 14:15-17) With the Holy Spirit living in their hearts, they would never be alone.

One of my favorite passages of Scripture is Paul's bold statement that through God's Spirit, Christ lives in each of us who knows Him. Paul wrote:

"To them God has chosen to make known among the Gentiles the glorious riches of this mystery, which is Christ in you, the hope of glory" (Colossians 1:27).

In another letter, Paul described us as temples of the Holy Spirit because the Spirit resides in us. (1 Corinthians 6:18-20) Another passage tells us that God's Spirit understands our needs perfectly, and He is constantly praying for us. (Romans 8:26-27) Do you need a little encouragement from time to time? Then think about the awesome Spirit of Almighty God living inside of you, caring for you, guiding you, and constantly praying to the Father for you.
• How do you respond when you think about God's Spirit living inside of you? Does it encourage you or frighten you? Explain your answer.

_____

_____

_____

The Holy Spirit isn't just some kind of impersonal force. He is a person. He delights in our faith, and He grieves when we sin. The Holy Spirit helps us grow in our faith day by day in the same way we first trusted Christ for salvation: by faith. Paul told us:

"So then, just as you received Christ Jesus as Lord, continue to live in him, rooted and built up in him, strengthened in the faith as you were taught, and overflowing with thankfulness" (Colossians 2:6-7).
• We initially trusted Christ to forgive us for our sins. What are some things we trust Him for each day as we grow deeper and stronger in our relationship with Him? _____

_____

_____

_____

_____

Several passages in the New Testament describe the contrast between living for our selfish old natures and living to please God. In his letter to the Galatians, Paul talks about the results of giving in to the temptations of our sinful desires. Then he says if we follow Christ, resist Satan's lies, and trust God to guide and strengthen us, He will transform us. He wrote:

"But [in contrast to the acts of the sinful nature,] the fruit of the Spirit is love, joy, peace, patience, kindness, goodness, faithfulness, gentleness and self-control..." (Galatians 5:22-23).

These things don't happen by magic. They are created in us as we trust God's will and ways when we are tempted to be unloving, angry, anxious, mean, and all the other evidences of selfishness.

• What are some specific situations in your life where you need God's Spirit in you to transform your attitudes and actions? _____

_____

_____

_____

• Look at Ephesians 4:22-24 in the introduction to this lesson. According to this passage, what's God's part in producing change in our lives? What's our part? _____

_____

_____

_____

Overcoming Temptations

I remember seeing a sign that read: "Little sins lead to big trouble." That's true; but before sin gets a grip on us, we're faced with a choice:

a temptation to go in the right way or the wrong way. Temptation isn't sin. All of us experience it; even Jesus did when He was on earth. The issue is how we respond to temptation. What choices will we make?

James described the progression of giving in to temptation:

"...but each one is tempted when, by his own evil desire, he is dragged away and enticed. Then, after desire has conceived, it gives birth to sin; and sin, when it is full-grown, gives birth to death" (James 1:14-15).

There's nothing wrong with appreciating a beautiful woman or a handsome man, a fine car, new clothes, the praise that comes from accomplishment, or the joy of being accepted by others. But when our hearts become fixed on these things and we have to have them, then we've crossed the line. As James described, desire inflamed temptation, and temptation gave birth to sin.
• Describe where the line is crossed from temptation to sin in these areas:

—Attraction, lust, and sexual sin: _____
_____
_____

—Possessions: _____
_____
_____

—Acceptance by friends:_____
_____
_____

Prestige or status: _____

_____

_____

The people we hang around shape our responses to temptation. If they are wise people, they'll be good examples of living for God and avoiding the destruction caused by giving in to temptations. If they're foolish, they'll encourage you to give in; and in fact, they'll make fun of you if you don't.
• Who are some wise friends who are good examples of resisting temptations? _____

_____

_____

_____

• Who are some friends who encourage you to sin, make fun of you if you don't join them in sinning, or don't care what you do? _____

_____

_____

_____

Two passages of Scripture give us encouragement and direction for this problem. John told us the wonderful fact: ". . . the one who is in you [that's Christ] is greater than the one who is in the world [that's Satan and his lying demons]" (1 John 4:4). Paul made his instructions about temptations very clear when he wrote to Timothy: "Flee the evil desires of youth, and pursue righteousness, faith, love and peace, along with those who call on the Lord out of a pure heart" (2 Timothy 2:22).

Don't mess around with temptation. Don't see how close you can get before you sin. Get away from it! Run like crazy, and replace those attitudes and actions with things that build your faith and fulfill God's purposes in your life.

• What are some reasons we mess around with temptations instead of running from them? What are some results? _____

_____

_____

_____

• Name some specific ways you can—and need to—"flee the evil desires of youth." _____

_____

_____

_____

Confession and Repentance

One of the things I love about the Bible is that it's so relevant. It offers the most hope of anything in the world, but that hope is blended with rock-hard reality. In John's first letter, he told his readers he was writing to them so they could avoid sinning. ". . . But if anybody does sin, we have one who speaks to the Father in our defense—Jesus Christ, the Righteous One" (1 John 2:1). Even in our worst times, Jesus stands with us to forgive us and defend us. That's grace!

In our culture, we see sin depicted on television and hear it in our music all day every day. Our culture doesn't grieve over it; we delight in it! But God's Spirit grieves when we sin because He knows our selfishness is destructive to us and to others.

• What are some sins that are glorified on television and in music?

_____
_____
_____

• What are some of the tragic effects when people become numb to sin's destructiveness?_____

_____
_____
_____

Another verse in John's first letter is sometimes called "God's bar of soap." It describes the way you and I can experience cleansing from sin:

"If we confess our sins, he [Christ] is faithful and just and will forgive us our sins and purify us from all unrighteousness" (1 John 1:9).

The word confession means "to agree with." When we confess our sins, we agree with God that, yes, that attitude or action was wrong. We agree with Him that Christ's death on the cross has already paid for that sin, and we agree that the best path for our lives is to avoid that sin in the future by repenting: turning away from sin and toward godliness. These wonderful truths mean we can be ruthlessly honest about our selfish, sinful hearts because God's forgiveness is so rich, deep, and wonderful.

• As you've been working through this lesson, has the Holy Spirit tapped you on the shoulder to remind you of sinful attitudes or actions in your life? If He has, write them here (write in code if you don't want anybody to be able to read it). If not, take some time to be quiet before God and ask Him to reveal anything in your life that doesn't please Him. If He reveals anything to you, write those here (in code, of course). _____

_____

_____

_____

• Now, agree with God that each of these things are, indeed, sin. Agree with Him that Christ's death has already paid for these sins, and strike through each one of them one by one as you thank God for His great forgiveness. _____

_____

_____

_____

• It's time to repent. What are some specific things you can do to avoid this sin next time and replace it with good and godly influences, behaviors, and attitudes? _____

_____

_____

_____

Wrap It Up
• What truths in this lesson have encouraged you the most? _____

_____

_____

_____

_____

• How have the principles about the role of the Holy Spirit, overcoming temptation, and confession helped your faith grow stronger? _____

_____

_____

_____

• Are there some questions that have come to mind during this lesson? Write them here. Who can give you wise input about these questions?

_____

_____

_____

CONNECTING WITH GOD

The more we understand about the incredible greatness of God and the sinfulness of our own hearts, the more we will marvel at the opportunity that He has given us to connect with Him through prayer. He's the Creator of the universe. He spoke and billions and billions of stars were thrown into space. The distances between stars are measured in hundreds, thousands, millions, and even billions of light-years. He is awesome beyond anything we can imagine—but He invites us to call Him "Abba, Father," which means "Daddy."

As we stay connected with God by talking and listening, He directs us to find and fulfill His purpose for our lives. His Word, the Bible, becomes rich and real as His Spirit opens our hearts to grasp its message. We sense God's presence and power to transform our lives and the lives of others.

Christ's life was filled with prayer. Mark's gospel recorded an instance that was probably repeated many times. He wrote, "Very early in the morning, while it was still dark, Jesus got up, left the house and went off to a solitary place, where he prayed" (Mark 1:35). If Jesus felt the need to connect with the Father, how much do you and I need to connect with Him in prayer?

Prayer doesn't "work" because we use some magic formula or particular words. We simply talk to the One who made us, bought us, and loves us. We can be completely honest because He already knows everything about us. We don't come with a grocery list of wants. Instead we go to God as grateful children who have been rescued from hell, adopted into His family, and blessed beyond our wildest dreams! And if we're smart, we'll learn to listen to Him.

This lesson looks at the patterns that guide our prayers, God's promises, and a few problems we may encounter.

Patterns of Prayer

In those last hours before He was arrested, tried, and murdered, Jesus gave some important lessons to His men. In the span of only a short time, He told them over and over again about the power of prayer. In fact, Jesus promised them twice in one statement:

"And I will do whatever you ask in my name, so that the Son may bring glory to the Father. You may ask me for anything in my name, and I will do it" (John 14:13-14).

Wow! That sounds like a blank check! "Anything"? Really? Yes, it's an incredible promise; but we need to understand what it means to pray "in Jesus' name." This phrase is packed with meaning. It provides three conditions. To pray in Jesus' name, we have to pray as His child, in His will, and for His glory. First, we have to be saved: in right standing before God based on the forgiveness only God can give. Then, our desires must be aligned with God's will. Finally, our motives need to be fixed on God's glory, not how cool people will think we are when we tell them God answered our prayer. If our prayer meets those conditions, then Jesus promises He'll answer...in His timing.

• You've probably heard people say "in Jesus' name" at the end of their prayers. Now that you understand what it means, how will these three conditions affect how you use that phrase? _____

_____

_____

Paul sprinkled his letters to churches with rich, wonderful prayers. These are great for us to think about and use to guide our prayers. One of my favorites is in his letter to the Colossians:

"...we have not stopped praying for you and asking God to fill you with the knowledge of his will through all spiritual wisdom and understanding. And we pray this in order that you may live a life worthy of the Lord and may please him in every way: bearing fruit in every good work, growing in the knowledge of God" (Colossians 1:9-10).

• Why do you think Paul's first priority in his prayer was to ask God to fill them with His wisdom? _____

_____

_____

As our relationship with God grows, we'll want every minute, every word, and every action to please Him. We'll see fear, unbelief, and selfishness in our lives; and we'll want God to root out those things. David had that attitude when he prayed,

"Search me, O God, and know my heart; test me and know my anxious thoughts. See if there is any offensive way in me, and lead me in the way everlasting" (Psalm 139:23-24).

• Is this the kind of prayer you really want to say to God? Why or why not? _____

_____

_____

Though there are no magic formulas and countless Christians have found meaning in any number of ways to pray, many have been encouraged by a simple acronym: ACTS, which stands for adoration, confession, thankfulness, and supplication (asking God to meet needs). When we don't know what or how to pray, this pattern can get us going and provide encouragement for us to connect with God in a meaningful way.
• Try it right now. Take a few minutes for...
—Adoration: Reflect on God's greatness and love;
—Confession: Be honest about any sin the Holy Spirit brings to mind, and agree with Him about it;
—Thankfulness: Express your gratitude to God for all the things He's done in your life and the lives of those you love; and
—Supplication: Bring your needs to God, and pray specifically in Jesus' name (as His child, in His will, and for His glory).

Promises

Peter described God's promises in the Bible as "very great and precious" (2 Peter 1:4). If we are aware of them, we can claim them and trust God to provide for us. I want to outline just a few of the many promises in God's Word:
—In Romans 8:32, Paul says if God did the ultimate for us (Christ came to earth and died to pay for our sins), then certainly we can be sure He will provide anything else we need.
—To the Philippians, Paul said God is capable of providing for us abundantly. He wrote, "And my God will meet all your needs according to his glorious riches in Christ Jesus"(Philippians 4:19).
—James recognized that all of us desperately need God's wisdom; but when we ask, we need to believe He will provide it for us. He wrote: "If

any of you lacks wisdom, he should ask God, who gives generously to all without finding fault, and it will be given to him. But when he asks, he must believe and not doubt..." (James 1:5-6).

—John wrote: "This is the confidence we have in approaching God: that if we ask anything according to his will, he hears us. And if we know that he hears us—whatever we ask—we know that we have what we asked of him" (1 John 5:14-15).

• What are some ways that trusting in these promises (and many others) would affect your prayer life? _____

_____

_____

_____

• How can you apply these promises to situations in your life right now? _____

_____

_____

_____

Some Problems in Prayer

Sometimes we're convinced that we're praying according to God's will, but we get a "no" instead of a "yes" from God. At other times, we pray for weeks, months, or even years about a particular need; but heaven seems to have a "Closed" sign on it. Sometimes we feel the joy of God's presence as we pray; but at other times, we feel distant and alone. What's the deal? What causes these problems, and what are some solutions?

Many of our questions about prayer are answered when we take time to reflect on the conditions of praying "in Jesus' name." Quite often, we realize we care more about our wants than about God's will; or we want God to answer, so we can brag about it to our friends. James talked about that issue when he wrote:

"You want something but don't get it... You do not have, because you do not ask God. When you ask, you do not receive because you ask with wrong motives, that you may spend what you get on your pleasures" (James 4:2-3).

Jesus pointed out another possible reason for our prayers not being answered. He said if we are bitter toward anyone, God may not answer our prayers until we've forgiven that person. (Mark 11:25)

Another reason God may not answer our prayers is that His timing isn't right. We have a need, a desire, a passion for the answer; but God can see the whole sweep of time and all of the people involved. He may be orchestrating situations to answer our prayer, but those situations may take time to develop.
• If and when you struggle with unanswered prayer, how can you use these insights to help you understand the cause? What are some ways that understanding might help you trust God more during those times? _____

_____

_____

Another, and very common, problem is that we're simply too busy to pray. That's just an excuse—and a bad one, too! The fact is we make time for anything that's important to us. We prioritize things in our lives all day every day. The excuse of not having time to pray simply means we've determined that other things are more important.

We need to be reminded that prayer isn't just a dull, boring exercise meant to numb our minds into mush. If that's what we think, we've forgotten how wonderful God's grace is, how vast His resources are, and how much He loves us. If we have even the slightest clue, we'll be desperate to spend more time with God... because He loves us and because we need Him.

• Take a look at your life and your priorities. How important is prayer to you right now? How important do you want it to be?

_____

_____

_____

One of the best ways to develop your prayer life is to find a group of Christian friends and pray together on a regular basis. Find time to be together and seek God's face. Thank Him for His grace toward you, and plead with Him to change lives. You'll never be the same—and neither will your friends or the people you pray for. _____

_____

_____

_____

Wrap It Up

• What truths in this lesson have encouraged you the most? _____

_____

_____

_____

• How have the principles about the patterns of prayer, God's promises,

_____

and the problems you might experience helped your faith grow
stronger? _____
_____
_____

• Are there some questions that have come to mind during this lesson?
Write them here. Who can give you wise input about these questions?
_____
_____
_____

LIGHT SABER

Over the years, a lot of excited people have come up to me and said things like: "Rick, you won't believe how much I'm learning from the Bible! It's like every verse is reading my mind. I can't put it down because I'm enjoying it so much!"

I've also seen people who looked like they just slipped into a coma when the Bible was being taught. Exciting? No, they see God's Word as a gigantic sleeping pill.

What's the difference? Why do some of us get so much out of reading the Bible, but others are bored senseless? The answer is in our expectations. We generally get what we expect to get out of it. If we see it as a massive textbook written by nomadic shepherds in a desert before the earth's crust hardened, we won't believe their words have any meaning for you and me in our fast-paced technological age. But if we believe these verses are God's very words—to you and me, personally, then we'll eagerly soak up every verse and treasure every point.

Treasures, though, are often hidden. They require some searching, some effort, and some tenacity. When we find that treasure, the value is so great that all of our efforts are richly rewarded. It's worth it!

The Bible calls itself a source of "light" to guide us and a "sword" we can use to fight spiritual battles. Like a traveler on a dark night, we desperately need light to know which direction to go. Like a warrior, we have to have a sharp weapon (and the skill to use it) to fight effectively. In this lesson, we'll look at the awesome power of God's Word, our decision to respond in faith, and how to go deeper than we've ever gone before in understanding the truths we find there.

The Power of God's Word

God's Spirit uses God's Word to change lives. We understand the Gospel message about Christ's offer of salvation by looking at passages of Scripture; and we grow in our faith as we increasingly grasp biblical truths about God, His purposes, and ourselves. Let's look at a few passages about the power of God's Word.

In Psalm 119:105, David said to God, "Your word is a lamp to my feet and a light for my path."

• What are some decisions you will face in the next few weeks? How can truths and principles from God's Word help you choose the right path? _____

_____

_____

The writer to the Hebrews boldly wrote to us: "For the word of God is living and active. Sharper than any double-edged sword, it penetrates even to dividing soul and spirit, joints and marrow; it judges the thoughts and attitudes of the heart. Nothing in all creation is hidden from God's sight. Everything is uncovered and laid bare before the eyes of him to whom we must give account" (Hebrews 4:12-13).

• What do you think this passage means? Is it encouraging or threatening to you? Explain your answer. _____

_____

_____

Again, David wrote in Psalm 119 to tell us that understanding God's truth is worth more than any other kind of riches: "... I love your commands more than gold, more than pure gold" (Psalm 119:127).
• What might cause the writer of this psalm to treasure God's Word so much? _____

_____

_____

_____

Peter understood how much young believers need God's Word. He wrote, "Like newborn babies, crave pure spiritual milk, so that by it you may grow up in your salvation" (1 Peter 2:2).
• What are some reasons we would genuinely "crave" truth from God's Word? _____

_____

_____

_____

Paul tells us the size of our faith depends on the depth of our understanding of God's Word. He wrote, "...faith comes from hearing the message, and the message is heard through the word of Christ" (Romans 10:17).
• Explain the direct link between our study of Scripture and the size of our faith. _____

_____

_____

_____

Our Decision to Respond

If we read the Bible without a commitment to respond to the truths we uncover, it becomes dry and boring. Before we read, we need to make a decision to respond to God in faith and in action.

As Joshua entered a new and challenging phase of his life, the Lord told him: "Be strong and very courageous. Be careful to obey all the law my servant Moses gave you.... Do not let this Book of the Law depart from your mouth; meditate on it day and night, so that you may be careful to do everything written in it. Then you will be prosperous and successful" (Joshua 1:7-8).

• What was God's promise to Joshua if he would study and follow His Word? _____

_____

_____

If we read but don't obey God's directions in the Scriptures, we aren't really following Him. Jesus explained this principle to the religious leaders:

"To the Jews who had believed him, Jesus said, 'If you hold to my teaching, you are really my disciples. Then you will know the truth, and the truth will set you free' " (John 8:31-32).

• On a scale of 0 (not at all) to 10 (completely), how much would you say you are "holding to [Christ's] teaching" by obeying His commands you find in Scripture? Explain your answer. _____

_____

_____

_____

In the last few hours with His disciples, Jesus told them: "If you remain in me and my words remain in you, ask whatever you wish, and it will be given you. This is to my Father's glory, that you bear much fruit, showing yourselves to be my disciples" (John 15:7-8).

• According to this passage, what factors are necessary for us to bear much fruit? What does it mean for Christ's words to "remain in you"?

_____

_____

_____

Going Deeper

Paul told the Colossians: "Let the word of Christ dwell in you richly..." (Colossians 3:16). Some of us have studied the Bible so much and so well that the riches of biblical insights are available all day every day in our memory banks. When we talk to people, we weave these life-changing truths into our conversations. When we pray, we are guided by what we know of God's will and God's ways from our Bible study. As we make decisions, we remember principles that shape our choices and keep us walking along the right path.

But the Bible is a huge book! Where do you start? How can you dig in and study something so massive? The very best way I've found to study God's Word is by using the pattern in Paul's second letter to Timothy. Paul wrote his young disciple:

"All Scripture is God-breathed and is useful for teaching, rebuking, correcting and training in righteousness, so that the man [or woman] of God may be thoroughly equipped for every good work" (2 Timothy 3:16-17).

I sometimes read a book of the Bible—like John or Ephesians or

1 Peter; and in fact, I read it two or three times. Then when I see a particular paragraph I want to dig into, I use four questions based on the passage from 2 Timothy:

—What does this passage teach me?

I observe who, where, when, what, and why in the verses; and I ask, "What is the author trying to communicate to his original audience?" This exploration may take me fifteen to thirty minutes.

—Where do I fall short of this teaching?

I ask the Lord to show me how my life doesn't match up with His character of love and strength, His purposes, and His ways described in this passage of Scripture. This part is painful, but it's absolutely necessary for repentance to take place.

—How can I correct my attitude or actions?

This part is usually pretty easy to define but difficult to achieve. It requires a clear plan of action and the courage to take those steps.

—How can I make this change a permanent part of my life?

The real fruit of this kind of study is not that I make a change once but that this change becomes a part of my life. In most cases, I memorize a verse or two and think often during the next week or so about how to apply that verse to the specific situations that surfaced when I focused on correction.

One more thing: For this kind of study to be as effective as possible, I need to write it out. There's something powerful about writing my thoughts that sharpens my mind and opens my heart. I know it's not magic, but it sure is effective! I encourage you to use a notepad or a notebook. Carve out thirty minutes or so each week to do this kind of study. During the rest of the week, read and pray; but at least once a week, dig deeper into God's Word in real Bible study.

Now it's your turn. Pick a passage of Scripture we've looked at in this or previous lessons, or choose one that has been meaningful to you in the past. If nothing comes to mind, look at Colossians 3:12-17.

If you picked a single verse, read the paragraph where it's found three or four times. Then answer these questions:

• What does this passage teach me? (Observe: who, where, when, what, and why. Also ask, "What does this passage mean?") _____

_____

_____

_____

• Where do I fall short of this teaching? _____

_____

_____

• How can I correct my attitude or actions? _____

_____

_____

• How can I make this change a permanent part of my life? _____

_____

_____

Wrap It Up

• What truths in this lesson have encouraged you the most? _____

_____

_____

_____

• How have the principles about the power of God's Word, the decision to respond in faith, and the process of going deeper helped your faith grow stronger? _____

_____

_____

• Are there some questions that have come to mind during this lesson? Write them here. Who can give you wise input about these questions?

_____

_____

_____

UNTIL THE WHOLE WORLD KNOWS

For a very good reason, Christ's death on the cross to pay for our sins is called a "ransom." We were helpless hostages with no hope to be free on our own. We were under the sentence of death, but Jesus Christ became our substitute and died in our place. If you and I have the slightest clue about what Jesus did for us, we'll be the most thankful people the world has ever known! We'll also tell every person who will listen about Him!

There aren't many things we can do here on earth that are better than they will be in heaven, but there's at least one: telling lost people about Christ. We have an incredible opportunity to be Christ's ambassadors. We are citizens of heaven, living in a foreign land and representing the King of kings.

One of the factors that gives Christians a razor's-edge sense of purpose is that we can see people from an eternal perspective. Paul wrote to the Corinthians: "So from now on we regard no one from a worldly point of view. Though we once regarded Christ in this way, we do so no longer" (2 Corinthians 5:16). Now we see people the way God sees them: as either children of God destined for heaven or lost, helpless souls headed toward eternal torment in hell. C. S. Lewis also once remarked if we see people in heaven with all their beauty and glory that we'd be tempted to worship them; but those in hell would be so repulsive that we'd turn away in horror. That's an eternal perspective about people you and I meet every day!

In this last lesson, we'll focus on the realities of being lost and found—the heart of the Gospel message—and how to tell others about our personal experience with Christ.

Lost and Found

We live in a world of riches and pleasure. Sure, we have tough times every now and then; but we are the richest and most comfortable people the world has ever known. With all of our riches, it's hard to realize a day is coming when people will be held accountable for turning their backs on Christ.

The same thing happened in the days of Noah. For a hundred years, he built his boat and listened to neighbors laugh at him for being so foolish in following a God they couldn't see. But then the bottom dropped out of the sky; and they drowned, experiencing the consequences for their sin. In the same way, our culture is cruising along, enjoying the benefits of enormous wealth; but someday things are going to change. Paul told the people in Thessalonica about a day that's coming:

"He [Christ] will pay back trouble to those who trouble you.... This will happen when the Lord Jesus is revealed from heaven in blazing fire with his powerful angels. He will punish those who do not know God and do not obey the gospel of our Lord Jesus. They will be punished with everlasting destruction and shut out from the presence of the Lord and from the majesty of his power on the day he comes to be glorified in his holy people and to be marveled at among all those who have believed..." (2 Thessalonians 1:6-10).

• In your own words, describe what that event will look like. Include a description of Jesus, His angels, and those who have rejected Christ.

_____

_____

_____

• Do you really believe this day will come? If so, how does it affect your attitude and behavior toward those who don't know Christ? _____

_____

_____

_____

In contrast, those who have trusted Christ (and who trust Him in the future) will enjoy the incredible blessings of heaven. In fact, heaven will be so wonderful, the biblical writers seem to have had a hard time describing what it will be like. They talk about us being tremendously thankful, enjoying being in the presence of God Almighty, and surrounded by enough gold and jewels to sink a fleet of battleships! In fact, the gold and precious stones we treasure so highly today will be so common in heaven that they'll be used for road and building materials!

In Revelation, John described heaven in glowing terms. Near the end of this book, he wrote,

"...'Now the dwelling of God is with men, and he will live with them. They will be his people, and God himself will be with them and be their God. He will wipe every tear from their eyes. There will be no more death or mourning or crying or pain, for the old order of things has passed away' " (Revelation 21:3-4).

• What aspects of heaven do you most look forward to? Explain your answer. _____

_____

_____

_____

The Heart of the Gospel

Over and over again, New Testament writers describe the basis of our relationship with God. They say we were lost, but Jesus found us. We were destined for hell, but Christ ransomed us and brought us back. We were helpless and hopeless in our sins, but Christ paid the price for us. We were dead, but He gave us life.

In his first letter to the Corinthians, Paul wanted them to understand the Gospel with absolute clarity. He wrote to them:

"Now, brothers, I want to remind you of the gospel I preached to you, which you received and on which you have taken your stand. By this gospel you are saved, if you hold firmly to the word I preached to you. Otherwise, you have believed in vain. For what I received I passed on to you as of first importance: that Christ died for our sins according to the Scriptures, that he was buried, that he was raised on the third day according to the Scriptures, and that he appeared to Peter, and then to the Twelve. After that, he appeared to more than five hundred of the brothers at the same time..." (1 Corinthians 15:1-6).

Paul explained there are two aspects of the Gospel: Christ's death on the cross that paid for our sins and His resurrection that gives us new life. The proof that Jesus died is that He was buried. (Living people aren't buried, you know.) The proof that Jesus was raised from the dead is that so many people—as many as five hundred at one time—were eyewitnesses who saw Him. Five hundred witnesses to an event would be powerful evidence in any courtroom!

• Imagine sitting in church in Corinth and hearing Paul's letter read for the first time. How do you think you would have responded to this passage? _____

_____

_____

_____

The most complete and comprehensive explanation of the Gospel in all of Scripture is in Romans. For several chapters, Paul outlines our need for a Savior, Christ's payment for sins, and what it means to be saved. When we want to explain the Gospel to someone, we can use selected verses from Paul's letter known as "The Roman Road" to salvation:

—**Romans 3:23:** "for all have sinned and fall short of the glory of God."

—**Romans 5:8:** "But God demonstrates his own love for us in this: While we were still sinners, Christ died for us."

—**Romans 6:23:** "For the wages of sin is death, but the gift of God is eternal life in Christ Jesus our Lord."

—**Romans 10:13:** " 'Everyone who calls on the name of the Lord will be saved.' "

• Think carefully about each of these verses. Then put each one in your own words:

—Romans 3:23: _____

_____

_____

—Romans 5:8: _____

_____

_____

—Romans 6:23: _____

_____

_____

—Romans 10:13: _____

_____

_____

Your Story

Jesus gave sight to a blind man; and when the Jewish leaders challenged this man, he simply told them: "Once I was blind, but now I see." That simple statement is a testimony of what Christ had done in his life. In the same way, Paul often told people about how he became a Christian in clear, simple terms. He explained what his life was like before he met Christ. Then he told the specifics of his encounter with Jesus and how he believed in Him. Next he mentioned some changes Christ made in his life. (Please see Acts 22:3-16 and Acts 26:8-18.)

Your testimony is a powerful tool to touch people's hearts. Take a few minutes to outline the specifics of your salvation story.

• What was your life like before you met Christ? Describe your sense of emptiness or rebellion or apathy toward God. Can you look back and see that God was trying to get your attention during this time? If so, describe God's attempts and your response. _____

_____

_____

• Describe the situation when you trusted Christ as your Lord and Savior. Who was there? What was said and done? How did God work in your heart? What caused you to "turn the corner" and trust in Him? Specifically, what did you say to Christ to express your trust in Him?

_____

_____

_____

• What are some changes God has made in your life since you trusted Christ? Describe the most significant changes in your attitude, mood, relationships, purpose in life, and desires. Focus on one of these and describe it in detail. _____

_____

_____

To the Whole World!

After Jesus told His disciples to go to the whole world to share the Gospel and make disciples, He gave them a strategy. He told them:

"But you will receive power when the Holy Spirit comes on you; and you will be my witnesses in Jerusalem, and in all Judea and Samaria, and to the ends of the earth" (Acts 1:8).

The strategy is for us first to go to our own "Jerusalem," our family and close friends, to tell them about Christ. Then we go a little farther to our "Judea and Samaria," our neighbors and our community. Finally, we do whatever we can—by praying, giving, or going—to reach every person in even the remotest parts of the globe because Jesus died for them, too!

• Who are the people in your "Jerusalem"? List them and pray for each one to come to know Christ. When and how will you talk to each of them? _____

_____

_____

• Who are the people in your "Judea and Samaria"? Pray for them. What are some ways you and other Christians can make contact with them to share the Gospel? _____

_____

_____

_____

• How is your church involved in reaching people "to the ends of the earth" for Christ? What are some ways you can pray specifically, give generously, or go to tell them about Jesus? _____

_____

_____

The famous missionary to China, Hudson Taylor, once said, "The Great Commission is not an option to be considered but a command to be obeyed." Successful witnessing is as much your responsibility as it is God's. Remember that success in witnessing is sharing the Gospel clearly in the power of the Holy Spirit and leaving the results to God.
• How does that definition of "successful witnessing" encourage you? How does it challenge you? _____

_____

_____

_____

Wrap It Up

• What truths in this lesson have encouraged you the most? _____

_____

_____

_____

• How have the principles about heaven and hell, the heart of the Gospel, and your testimony helped your faith grow stronger? _____

_____

_____

_____

• Are there some questions that have come to mind during this lesson? Write them here. Who can give you wise input about these questions?

_____

_____

_____

ABOUT RICK GAGE

In 1986, Rick Gage walked away from a promising career coaching football and surrendered his life to full-time evangelistic ministry. A few years later, he became the founder of Rick Gage Ministries. He has been conducting evangelistic events around the world and has seen tens of thousands make commitments to the Lord Jesus Christ.

Roger Alford of the Associated Press wrote, "Gage fills stadiums just as full as the Rev. Billy Graham does. It's just that the stadiums are much smaller. The Texas native takes his Go Tell Crusades to the small towns that other preachers might see only from the air on their way to big cities. Like Graham, Gage preaches the same Gospel, offers the same invitation to would-be believers, and sees multitudes walk toward the platform to accept Christ."

Rick is also the founder of GO TELL Ministries. His annual GO TELL Youth Camps, which began in 1989, have reached tens of thousands of students and their leaders from churches across the country. These summer camps have helped thousands of students come to Christ or surrender to full-time ministry.

To further impact the youth of America, Rick has delivered his nationally acclaimed "ON TRACK" assembly program to more than 2 million teenagers in our nation's schools. This program confronts young people's abuse of drugs and alcohol. In addition, he has appeared on numerous radio and television programs. He is the author of his autobiography, *More Than a Game*, and a Bible study, *Download*, which helps people grow in their faith.

For fun, Rick enjoys jogging, working out, and hunting. Rick, his wife Lynne, and their daughters Sara and Anna live near Atlanta, Georgia.

ABOUT RICK GAGE MINISTRIES

Educators, coaches, pastors, city officials, sports personalities, and politicians nationwide have acclaimed Rick Gage's profound impact on young people. He is considered an authority on youth culture and the pressures faced by today's students.

Rick has spoken face-to-face to more than 2 million students in America's public schools through his nationally acclaimed ON TRACK assembly program. This hard-hitting, honest talk on the realities of life among today's youth has transformed the attitudes and destinies of hundreds of thousands of young people in the United States.

As one of today's most sought-after youth communicators, Rick is also an internationally known evangelist. He has led thousands of people—young and old, rich and poor of all ethnic backgrounds—to make personal decisions to live for Christ.

God has given Rick a tremendous vision to fulfill the Great Commission. As a result of this vision, the Rick Gage Evangelistic Association was founded in 1990 with its headquarters in the Atlanta area. Other ministries of this evangelistic association include:

GO TELL Crusades in football stadiums, drawing thousands from cities and surrounding regions for a major evangelistic event.

GO TELL Youth Camps, attracting tens of thousands of students and youth leaders from churches nationwide to be equipped in evangelism and discipleship.

A strategic international ministry, reaching into the former Soviet Union. An estimated 500,000 Russian Bibles and Christian books—as well as tons of humanitarian aid and medical supplies—have been distributed. As a result of these efforts, thousands of Russians have committed their lives to Christ.

Rick Gage Ministries constantly has new opportunities to present  the Good News of Jesus Christ, and we praise Him for the many lives we continue to see changed by His power. With the Apostle Paul, we say, "...pray for us that the message of the Lord may spread rapidly and be honored, just as it was with you" (2 Thessalonians 3:1).

As you've been reading this book, perhaps God has touched your heart and you'd like to help this ministry accomplish the mission God has given to us. Rick Gage Ministries is a nonprofit organization. If you'd like to contribute to our ministry of reaching the lost and changing lives, send a tax-deductible donation to Rick Gage Ministries. We'd really appreciate it! And if you have any questions about how you can contribute regularly, contact us by phone, mail, or email.

For more information, please visit our web site at: rickgageministries.com

CONTACT US

WE WANT TO HEAR FROM YOU!

You may have questions about your relationship with Christ, or you may just want to tell us what God has done in your life. Maybe you want to ask us to pray for you, or maybe you feel you are at the end of the road and you have no one else to turn to. Whatever the reason, please contact us. We'd love to hear from you.

Find us on the web at:

rickgageministries.com

Email us at:

info@rickgageministries.com

Or mail to:

Rick Gage Ministries
P.O. Box 2138
Duluth, GA 30096

A NOTE FROM RICK

Welcome to the Rick Gage Ministries family! I want you to know we are praying for you. I hope you will continue to pray for my family, this ministry, and me as we take the message of Christ to people all over America and around the world.

If this book has spoken to your heart or you have specific prayer needs, please contact us. We'll join you in bringing your needs before the Throne of Grace. God bless you!

"I thank my God every time I remember you. In all my prayers for all of you, I always pray with joy" (Philippians 1:3-4).

TO ORDER
MORE COPIES...

Thousands of people are gaining insight into their relationship with Christ from *Download*. Many are using it to study the Bible and apply life-changing truths on their own, but many more are using it for stimulating group study and discussions. If you, your friends and family, and your church need more copies, give us a call!

To order more copies of *Download*...
Go online to www.rickgageministries.com
Or write to:
    Rick Gage Ministries
    P.O. Box 2138
    Duluth, GA 30096

Discounts		S&H
1 book............$4.95		$1/book
2-6 books.........$4.50/book		$0.75/book
7-12 books........$4.00/book		$0.50/book
Over 12 books....$3.50/book		$0.40/book

ORDER INFORMATION

Number of books: [   ]

$ [   ] per book

Subtotal $ [   ]

Shipping per book: $ [   ]

Shipping Total $ [   ]

Grand Total: $ [   ]

Payment options:
Credit cards are accepted online.
Checks are accepted by mail.

ALSO AVAILABLE...

The story of Rick's career in football and how God changed his heart and the direction of his life. The book is called *More Than a Game.*

To order this book, go to the same website and find the price and shipping information.

NOTES

_____
_____
_____
_____
_____
_____
_____
_____
_____
_____
_____
_____
_____
_____
_____
_____
_____
_____
_____
_____
_____
_____
_____

DOWNLOAD